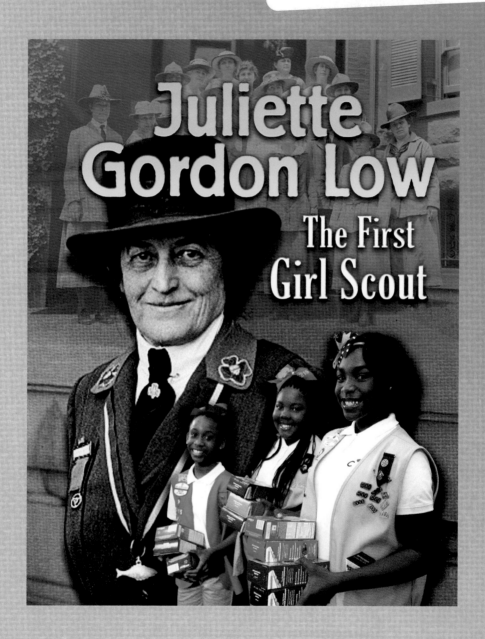

Juliette Gordon Low

The First Girl Scout

Dona Herweck Rice

Publishing Credits

Rachelle Cracchiolo, M.S.Ed., *Publisher*
Conni Medina, M.A.Ed., *Managing Editor*
Emily R. Smith, M.A.Ed., *Series Developer*
June Kikuchi, *Content Director*
Jordan Smith, *Assistant Editor*
Regina Frank, *Graphic Designer*

Image credits: front cover, p.1 Bettmann/Getty Images; front cover (bottom), p.1 A.M.P.A.S./PictureLux/Age Fotostock; front cover (background), p.1 Library of Congress [LC-DIG-hec-11048]; p.5 Greg E. Mathieson, Sr./REX/Shutterstock; p.6, p.7, p.13, p.18, p.19 (bottom), p.23, p.25 Public domain; p.9 David B. King (Creative Commons); p.15 Hulton Deutsch/Getty Images; p.17 Chronicle/Alamy; p.19 Look and Learn; p.20 Library of Congress [HABS GA,26-SAV,15-11]; p.21 (top) Library of Congress [LC-DIG-hec-09024]; p.21 (bottom) Courtesy of Georgia Historical Society, the Ann Mintz collection of Girl Scouts Troop 1 records, MS 2351; p.23 (bottom) FA2010 (Creative Commons); p.27 (top) Walter Oleksy/Alamy; p.27 (insert) Library of Congress [LC-USZ62-25808]; all other images from iStock and/or Shutterstock.

Library of Congress Cataloging-in-Publication Data

Names: Rice, Dona Herweck, author.
Title: Juliette Gordon Low : the first Girl Scout / Dona Herweck Rice.
Description: Huntington Beach, CA : Teacher Created Materials, [2019] | Includes index. | Audience: Grades K-3.
Identifiers: LCCN 2017057814 (print) | LCCN 2017058038 (ebook) | ISBN 9781493887828 (eBook) | ISBN 9781493887811 (pbk.)
Subjects: LCSH: Low, Juliette Gordon, 1860-1927--Juvenile literature. | Girl Scouts--United States--Biography--Juvenile literature.
Classification: LCC HS3359.L6 (ebook) | LCC HS3359.L6 R54 2018 (print) | DDC 369.463092 [B] —dc23

Teacher Created Materials

5301 Oceanus Drive
Huntington Beach, CA 92649-1030
www.tcmpub.com

ISBN 978-1-4938-8781-1

© 2018 Teacher Created Materials, Inc.
Printed in China
YiCai.032019.CA201901471

Table of Contents

On a Mission

The Girl Scouts have a big job to do!

The Scouts "build girls of courage, confidence, and character." Most of all, they want to "make the world a better place." These are the words of the Girl Scout Mission. This is why the Scouts do what they do.

Juliette Gordon Low founded, or started, the Girl Scouts. The Scouts began more than one hundred years ago. Low lived with courage, confidence, and character. She wanted to help girls around the world do the same. Millions of girls have done just that, thanks to the Girl Scouts. And the world is a better place for it!

Girl Scout Laws

The Girl Scouts have laws that the Scouts pledge to uphold. These include being honest, helpful, and caring. Scouts pledge to be strong and respectful too. Girl Scouts are meant to be good citizens and leaders.

Girl Scouts camp on the White House lawn with former President Barack Obama and Michelle Obama.

5

Daisy Sprouts

Juliette Gordon was born in 1860 in Georgia. It was Halloween day. Her uncle said she would be "a daisy." That meant a great person. The name stuck. She was called Daisy for the rest of her life.

Daisy's family was wealthy. Her father was William Gordon. He was from Georgia. Her mother was Eleanor Kinzie. She was from Chicago. Daisy was their second child. They would have four more.

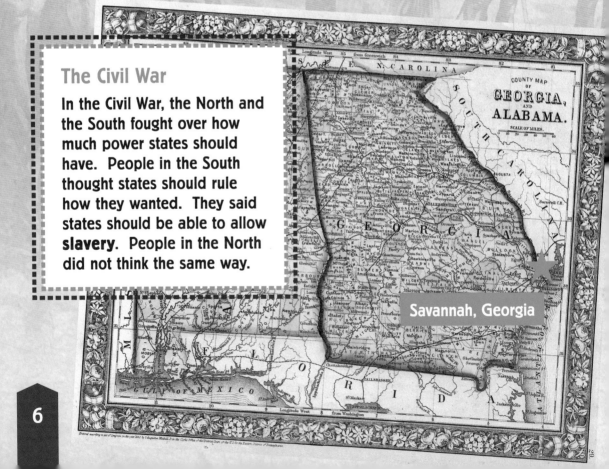

The Civil War

In the Civil War, the North and the South fought over how much power states should have. People in the South thought states should rule how they wanted. They said states should be able to allow **slavery**. People in the North did not think the same way.

Savannah, Georgia

Things were not easy for the family when Daisy was young. A fierce war had started. It was the Civil War between the North and the South. Some of the war was fought near Daisy's home. The Gordons lived in a city called Savannah. The city is in Georgia. Her father fought for the South during the war. Much of the family's **goods** were given to help soldiers. Many people who lived near the fighting had little to live on.

Juliette "Daisy" Gordon as a child

Going North

Daisy's grandfather was a friend of William T. Sherman. Sherman led the Northern army. He went to see Daisy's mother. He told her to take the children to the North. Savannah was not safe. So, they went to Chicago. Daisy thought her grandparents were her enemies because they lived in the North. But she was wrong. They were good people. Daisy learned to love them.

Finally, the war ended. Daisy and her family went home. They rebuilt their life bit by bit. They grew wealthy again.

The South was not the same. But Daisy's future was bright.

Sugar Snow

General Sherman gave the Gordon children sugar. It was the first time they had sugar. In Chicago, they saw snow for the first time. Daisy was sure it was sugar from the sky!

General William T. Sherman

Daisy and her siblings were active outdoors. They ran, climbed, swam, and rode horses. Daisy loved nature and all animals. She once risked her life to save a drowning kitten.

Daisy was bold and fearless. She did what was right no matter what. Sometimes that got her into trouble! That is why her siblings called her "Crazy Daisy."

Each summer, Daisy and her family went to an aunt's house in northern Georgia. Many of her relatives stayed there all summer long. The kids made crafts and played. They wrote a magazine, too. Daisy wrote and drew the art. She was a good artist. In fact, she made and loved art all her life.

Something for Everyone

Daisy liked doing things outdoors. She also loved writing and drawing. Later, she made sure Girl Scouts participated in those activities, too.

School Days

When Daisy was young, she went to school with her siblings. They learned to read and write. They also learned French, history, and math. They learned manners, too.

As a teen, Daisy was sent to **finishing school**. The school was for girls only. They were trained to be ladies. The girls had to stay quiet and not run outdoors. Girls were supposed to marry rich men one day and run wealthy households.

Daisy was lonely at school. She begged her sister Alice to join her. Alice did not want to go, but their mother said she should. Sadly, Alice got very ill at school and died. Daisy was heartbroken. But she finished school. The path for her life as a lady seemed set.

An Important Lesson

At home, Daisy went to Sunday school. Her teacher taught that all people are the same. She said to love everyone and treat them well. She once brought a guest from Japan so the children could see that all people are alike.

1887 oil painting of Daisy as a teenager

Daisy Blooms

Back home in Georgia, Daisy was very popular. She was full of life. A few young men wanted to marry her. Daisy fell in love with William Low. The two were wed on December 21, 1886. It was the same day her parents were married years before.

The couple moved to England. They lived well and had many houses and servants. But Daisy was not happy. Her husband drank too much and was often cruel. They had no children. This made Daisy sad. She adopted many pets to love and care for. She also tried to help those in need. She wanted her life to have purpose, or meaning.

Almost Deaf

As a child, Daisy got a bad earache. The treatment damaged the hearing in that ear. Then, on her wedding day, a grain of rice got stuck in the other ear. When the doctor tried to take the rice out, he damaged her hearing more.

Help for Daisy

The Lows were married for nearly 20 years. Then, William died. Daisy was just 45 years old. But his death was not the only shock. In his **will**, William left most of his money to someone else. Daisy was suddenly poor. Her parents helped her. Her friends helped her, too. Then, Daisy got a good **lawyer**. In time, the courts said that Daisy should have some of William's money and things. She was granted enough to live well for the rest of her life.

But Daisy still needed a purpose for her life. She found it when she met Sir Robert Baden-Powell.

Go Fish

After William died, Daisy grew more like her old self. She loved to fish. Sometimes she fished with the men after a fancy dinner. And she wore her evening gown to do it!

Sir Robert Baden-Powell

Girl Scouts

Daisy met Sir Robert at a party. She was fascinated as he told her about the Boy Scouts he had founded in England. At first, the boys helped out in wartime. They learned survival skills. They took an **oath** to be of service to those in need and to their country.

Daisy was inspired! She wanted to do the same thing for girls. Sir Robert told her about the Girl Guides his sister had started in England. Daisy chose to start a troop, or group, in Scotland. Seven poor girls came. Daisy fed them and taught them skills. Those skills helped the girls learn to provide for themselves.

Daisy started a second troop in London. She was eager to do more!

Sir Robert and Daisy

THE GIRL GUIDES

Every week on this page you will be able to see how things have changed across the years

A number of girls in uniform turned up at the first Boy Scout rally at Crystal Palace, London, in 1909, and demanded to join the scouts. The Chief Scout, Sir Robert Baden-Powell, agreed to start "Girl Guides."

Brownies are the junior branch of the Girl At first called "Rosebuds," they started in 19 younger sisters of the Guides clamoured to movement, too. Brownies are aged 7½ to

This drawing shows how the Girl Guides changed over the years.

A training centre in the New Forest called Foxlease was given to the Guides in 1922 by a Mrs. Archbold. The Princess Royal provided funds from her wedding-present money to train the guide leaders.

Until 1930 the Girl Guides Association had their offices in the Scout headquarters. The increasing expansion of the movement forced them to build their own premises in Buckingham Palace Road, London.

The Guide movement spread across the world. In 1930 the World Association was formed to link Girl countries. Later a World Flag and Badge members of the association.

One way in which the Guides could help their country during the two world wars was by collecting scrap paper. They did many other valuable jobs. By now the hat had been abandoned in favour of the beret.

Four thousand guides from all over the w a camp in Windsor Great Park in 1957 to the centenary of the birth of Lord Bade Chief Scout. Olave, Lady Baden-Powell, i

How Girls can Help TO BUILD UP THE Empire

THE HANDBOOK FOR GIRL GUIDES

BY MISS BADEN-POWELL AND SIR R. BADEN-POWELL

Daisy used this book to help write one for the Girl Scouts.

19

In 1912, Daisy told her friends in the United States that she had exciting news to share with them. She was going back to Georgia. She was ready to start the Girl Guides in her home city and state! Soon, she changed the name to the Girl Scouts.

Eighteen girls joined right away. They were the first Girl Scouts. They met once each week. At each meeting, they ate and were active outdoors. They also learned many skills. They learned everything from tying knots to cooking to first aid. When girls completed a skill, they earned a **badge**.

Daisy taught them the Girl Scout laws. The Scouts promised to do their duty and help other people. They followed these laws wherever they went.

History at Home

Savannah is home to the Juliette Gordon Low Historic District. Visitors can see where Daisy was born and lived as a child. They can also see her home from when she was an adult. They can visit the first Girl Scout **headquarters**.

Daisy (right) stands with some of her Girl Scouts. To date, nearly 60 million girls have been Scouts.

Girl Scouts Troop 1 formed a basketball team.

A New Purpose

Daisy found her purpose at last. The rest of her life was all about the Girl Scouts. She designed a **uniform** for the Scouts to wear. Daisy wore it, too. In fact, she wore it every day. She also donated a house as a place for the Scouts to meet.

Daisy loved the Scouts. She wanted all girls to benefit from scouting. She went around the country to tell people about the Scouts. She asked women to start more troops. She would not take no for an answer. If a woman tried to say no, Daisy pretended not to hear her! Soon, many Girl Scout troops started all over the country.

Artful

Daisy loved art and artists. She helped found the Savannah Art Club. The group supported the work of local artists. It brought artists from around the world to Georgia. When the Girl Scouts turned 100, the group had an art show with Daisy's art.

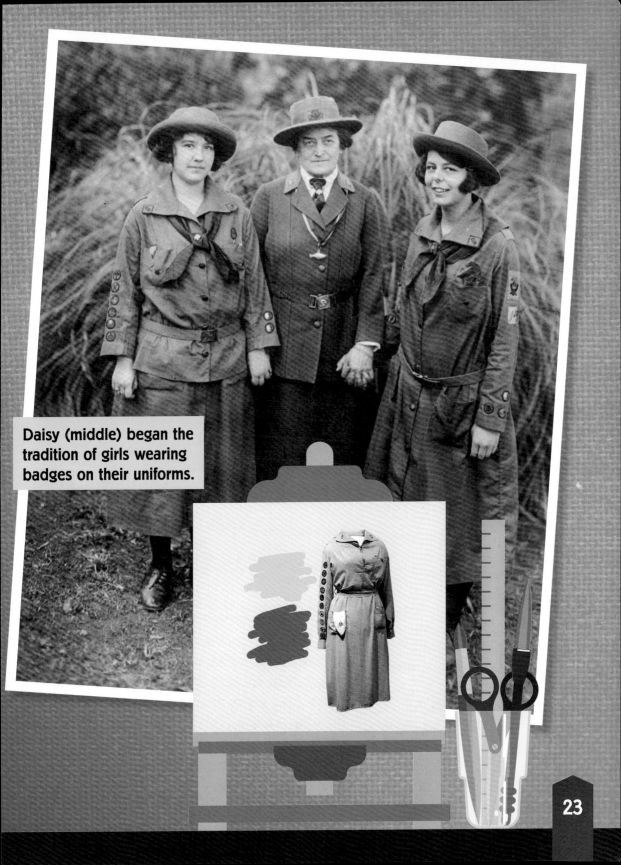

Daisy (middle) began the tradition of girls wearing badges on their uniforms.

Daisy founded the national Girl Scout organization so that all Scouts could learn the same things. They earned badges for skills. They served people in need. Thousands of girls joined.

Daisy and a friend also wrote a handbook for the Girl Scouts. It is filled with all sorts of information. How can you help someone with a broken bone? It is in the handbook. How can you read the stars? It is in there, too.

Daisy spent most of her days telling people about the Girl Scouts. She raised money for them. She talked to everyone she could.

When Daisy was not talking about the Scouts, she was visiting them. Daisy focused all her energy on the Girl Scouts.

Girl Scout Cookies

Girl Scouts are known for their cookies. The first cookie sales were in 1917. A troop baked cookies and sold them to raise money. For years after that, troops made and sold cookies. In 1936, the Girl Scouts began to sell boxed cookies made by **licensed** bakers.

Daisy pins an award on a Scout.

"Best Girl Scout"

Daisy was proud of her work. She used her place in **society** to help the Girl Scouts grow.

Daisy wanted to bring all Girl Scouts to a camp in New York. It would take a long time to build the camp. But Daisy did not have long. She was very sick and was dying.

The leaders of the Girl Scouts worked hard to get the camp ready. They succeeded. Daisy led the way! After the camp, the leaders sent Daisy a message. It said, "You are the best Girl Scout of them all."

Daisy died on January 17, 1927. She was buried in her uniform. The special message from the camp leaders was in her pocket.

Scouts gather for a meeting with Daisy.

First Lady of the Girl Scouts

In 1917, Daisy asked the **First Lady** to join the Girl Scouts. She asked her to be the honorary president. Edith Wilson (right) was the first to have this title. She helped the Girl Scouts grow. Since then, every U.S. first lady has held the title.

Make It!

A classic Girl Scout craft is the sit-upon. It is used for sitting on hard floors at meetings. It is also used outdoors at campsites. The sit-upon is usually waterproof.

You can make a sit-upon too!

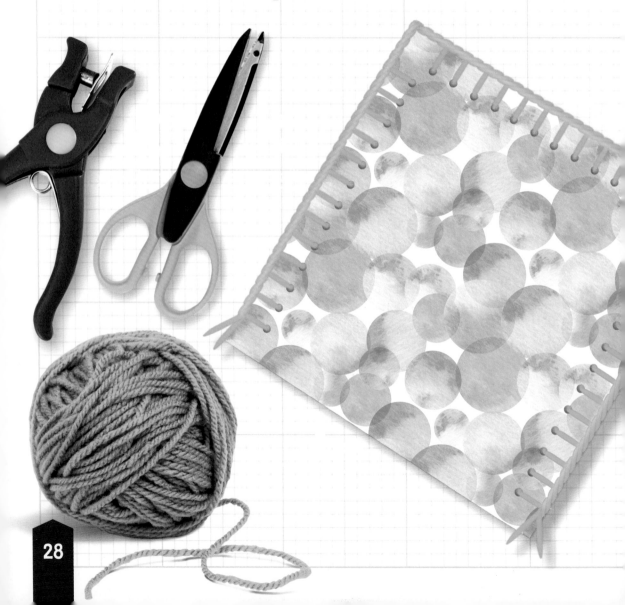

Materials

- old vinyl tablecloth or other waterproof material
- hole puncher
- scissors
- yarn
- plastic bags, shredded newspaper, or cotton stuffing

To Do

1. Cut a rectangle from the tablecloth. Make it twice the size you want for your sit-upon.

2. Fold the rectangle in half to make a square. The decorated sides should face out.

3. Punch holes about an inch apart around the three open sides of the square.

4. Line up the holes. Lace the yarn through the first hole, and tie it in place.

5. Stitch up and over, through the holes around two of the sides.

6. Fill the square with plastic bags or other stuffing.

7. Finish stitching the third side of the square. Tie off the end. Trim any loose yarn.

8. Sit on your sit-upon!

Glossary

badge—a cloth patch given to a person for doing a skill

finishing school—school where girls from wealthy families are taught proper behavior and manners

first lady—wife of the president of the United States

goods—things a person owns, especially food

headquarters—the main location of a group or organization

lawyer—a person whose job is to advise about legal rights

licensed—permitted to do something

oath—pledge or promise

slavery—a state of being owned by another person and forced to work without pay

society—the wealthy and powerful members of a community

uniform—standard clothing worn by all members of a group

will—legal document that outlines what a person wants done with his or her belongings after death

Index

Your Turn!

Girl Scouts earn badges for completing skills. They can get them for skills such as first aid or building a robot. Think of a special skill that you have. Design what the badge for the skill would look like. Write what someone would have to do to earn the badge.